AMERICAN BARNS

Jan Corey Arnett

SHIRE PUBLICATIONS

Published in Great Britain in 2013 by Shire Publications
Ltd, Midland House, West Way, Botley, Oxford OX2 0PH,
United Kingdom.

43-01 21st Street, Suite 220B, Long Island City, NY
11101, USA.

E-mail: shire@shirebooks.co.uk   www.shirebooks.co.uk

© 2013 Jan Corey Arnett.

A CIP catalog record for this book is available from the
British Library.

Shire Library no. 751.   ISBN-13: 978 0 74781 249 4

Jan Corey Arnett has asserted her right under the
Copyright, Designs and Patents Act, 1988, to be identified
as the author of this book.

Designed by Ken Vail Graphic Design and typeset in
Perpetua.

Printed in China through Worldprint Ltd.

13 14 15 16 17   10 9 8 7 6 5 4 3 2 1

COVER IMAGE
This 1882 three-story round barn near Twin Bridges,
Montana, was home to Spokane, the 1889 Kentucky
Derby winner. (Photograph by Jill Bayers Hotchkiss)

TITLE PAGE IMAGE
A well-kept American farm is a feast for the eye and the
camera lens.

CONTENTS PAGE IMAGE
The beauty of a Pennsylvania Mail Pouch barn is enriched
by autumn's glow.

ACKNOWLEDGEMENTS
My deepest gratitude goes to the many people who have
provided expertise and images for this book. Because
of you, American barns are being celebrated and saved.
Special thanks to Ric Beck, Lois Bolf, Charles Bultman,
Dawn Bonner, Patrick Branson, Ken Brock, Lisa Clark,
Keith Cramer, Jerry R. Davis, Ron Day, Robert DeBerry,
Lisa Duskin-Goede, Bill Ganzel, Robert A. Getzloff, Pamela
Whitney Gray, John Hallberg, Sally Hatcher, Jill Bayers
Hotchkiss, Greg Huber, Sonja Ingram, Aline Jannenga,
Brenda Keith, Kristin Kolkowski, Elizabeth Kostelny,
David Kusel, Charles Law, Randy Leffingwell, Charles Leik,
Shan Martin, Russ Mawby, Molly McDonald, Julia McGuire,
Marin Melchior, Chris Moore, Dan Myers, Linda Nycum,
Mark O'English, Thomas O'Grady, Wayne Olson,
Kathleen Paterka, Danae Peckler, Ned Pratt, Susan
Quinnell, Jon Radojkovic, Larry Rizor, Victoria Rocha,
Richard Roosenberg, Sunhi Ryan, James Scherrer, Dan
Schmitt, Nancy Sherbert, Bob Sherriff, Suzanne Stanis, John
Michael Vlach, Sarah Walker, Mark Whitney, Wade Wilcox,
and Kristen Young. Most of all, thanks to my husband, Doyle
Arnett, and sisters, Judy Cappiello and June Troyer.

PHOTOGRAPH ACKNOWLEDGEMENTS
Photographs are reproduced courtesy of: Dan Myers, 3;
Tillers International, 7 (left); Billy Graham Evangelistic
Association, 7 (right); Greg Huber, 10 (top); Lisa
Duskin-Goede, 12 (bottom); Ned Pratt, 13; Collection
of Charles Leik, 14 (top left); Mount Vernon Ladies'
Association, 14 (top right); Sonja Ingram, 16 (top);
Randy Leffingwell, 17, 27, 39; Vintage Aerial, 18 (top);
University of Vermont Morgan Horse Farm, 18 (middle);
Sherriff-Goslin Co, 19 (top); Ron Day, Ronday
Photography, 20; Kenneth and Mildred Corey family,
24 (top), 27 (inset), 31, 36 (top), 42 (bottom), 48 (top);
drawing by Jerry R. Davis, 24, (bottom); Institute for
Regional Studies & University Archives, North Dakota,
25; Wabaunsee County Historical Society, Kansas,
(the late Charles Herman), 26 (top); Wade Wilcox,
AmishCountryImages, 26 (bottom), 34, 47 (top);
Connecticut Trust for Historic Preservation, Historic
Barns of Connecticut Project, 30; Robert DeBerry, 37;
Kansas State Historical Society, 42 (top); Archives of the
State Historical Society of North Dakota, 48 (bottom);
Schussler Creative Inc., 50; Mauser Harmony with Nature
Foundation, Inc. William T. Cook, 55 (top); Julie McGuire,
Save Maplenol Barn, 56 (top); David Kusel, Manning
Heritage Foundation, 56 (bottom); Kristin Kolkowski,
Chase Stone Barn Committee, 59 (top and bottom);
All other images by the author.

Shire Publications is supporting the Woodland Trust, the UK's leading woodland conservation charity, by funding the dedication of trees.

CONTENTS

A BARN BY ANY OTHER NAME   4

THE HEART OF EVERY FARM   22

FORM, FIT, AND FUNCTION   32

BARNS IN DECLINE   40

WHEN EVERYTHING OLD IS NEW AGAIN   50

PLACES TO VISIT   62

GLOSSARY   68

FURTHER READING   70

INDEX   72

A BARN BY ANY OTHER NAME

A SK ANYONE in the United States to describe an American barn and the responses will vary. While much has been written about the American barn, there may be no singular structure that typifies it. The nation has an eclectic array of structures, many of which can legitimately be called barns. Some use the word to describe metal-sheathed buildings which arrived at around the time of World War II, but for the most part, a traditional barn is built of wood, or wood and stone. To the purist it must also be timber-framed (post and beam) and well braced or pegged since some early barns were built without the use of pegs.

Designs which traveled to the United States with immigrants from Europe and South America as far back as the 1600s have evolved to suit the purposes, landscape, location, and natural, financial, and technological resources of the American farmer.

Little information exists regarding what Native Americans—the first people known to call the continent home—used as barns. Resourceful and creative, most were nomadic out of necessity, so their dwellings and belongings had to be transportable. Apart from horses, livestock was rarely kept and crops fed a community for one season. Most structures sheltering humans were constructed of animal hides lashed to poles, referred to as tepees or wigwams. Permanent homes, such as those in Algonquin Indian towns of North Carolina, were lodges or longhouses, some having up to five rooms. They were made of bark, woven plant matter, and poles but unlike in parts of Europe, these were not generally shared with animals. Cliff dwellers of the southwest or mountainous populations kept supplies in caverns. Curious as it may seem, such places qualify as a barn if one accepts the broadest definition of the word as "a storage place." The word "barn" comes from the Old English *bere* (barley) and *aern* (place), meaning a place to store barley. In Anglo-Saxon England, it was precisely that—a building used for threshing and storing grain crops and. on occasion, to shear sheep. Cattle had a cowhouse, horses a stable, pigs a piggery, and equipment a cartshed.

Opposite:
The barn often used to depict an American farm structure is the red, gambrel-roofed dairy barn of the 1900s.

5

A longhouse at the Museum of Ojibwa Culture, St. Ignace, Michigan.

America's barns are diverse and beautiful. This Midwest barn and stone silo date to the early 1900s.

When colonization began on America's east coast in the early 1600s, two of the earliest distinct barn styles came from the English and the Dutch. The architecture of the Dutch barn is similar to that of European cathedrals dating back to the thirteenth century and to European tithe barns built to store portions of crops tithed to local churches. Common defining characteristics are high-pitched roofs, low eaves, horizontal siding, and

wagon doors at both gable ends. A Dutch barn frame also must have an "H-bent," formed of two large vertical posts and a horizontal round-ended cross-beam, connected with mortise and tenon joints, with the tenons protruding beyond the posts. An estimated 1,600 "New World Dutch Barns" were built, primarily in New York and New Jersey, before 1825. These are the nation's oldest post and beam barns.

Architecture aside, the awe that can be experienced inside a barn when light is streaming through windows and between boards evokes, for many, a spiritual feeling. Several churches across the United States began as barns. Conversely, some churches have become barns. And in some communities, barns still serve both purposes. Utah's Mormons do not use barns as places of worship but use a variety of buildings as tithe barns. Best known is the Lehi Ward Tithing Barn in Lehi, Utah, built in 1872. The Mormons are the only religious group known to use tithe barns in the United States.

Many barn enthusiasts agree that the English barn remains the most commonly seen barn in the United States, but with shingles or metal sheeting in place of traditional thatch roofing, and boards rather than stick and daub siding. But the interior configuration remained the same, using the three-bay, timber-frame layout for a structure generally 30 feet wide by about 40 feet long. They were initially built on the level. Later versions might be banked into a hill. Some researchers maintain that the banked barn is of German origin and that a banked English barn is an American alteration. German barns featured an asymmetrical roofline and made use of the hills of Bavaria and the Swiss Alps by being constructed so that the ridge line ran parallel to the hill with one side of the barn built into it. That has been done in the United States as well with crops stored on the main floor and animals kept below. A southern exposure is ideal. The German design has at least a pentice to protect the exposed wall, but many have a cantilevered overhang or forebay

Above left:
An English gable bank barn built in the 1870s, moved and restored 130 years later. The ornate cupola replicates the barn's original, but is not common to all English barns.

Above right:
The Billy Graham Library, Charlotte, North Carolina, a facility that carries on the message of Jesus Christ that American evangelist Billy Graham preached for more than sixty years, is styled after the beloved barn on his childhood North Carolina farm.

Above and left:
A classic Dutch barn in New York featuring distinctive H-bent framing.

Below:
The Community Church of Rolling Meadows, Illinois, called itself "The Church in a Barn" in the mid-1950s.

Above: A close look reveals a gambrel-roofed barn in church attire, home to the Pious Union of St. Joseph, Grass Lake, Michigan. The copper-roofed section is a later addition.

Below: "This is where I come to find God," is an expression familiar to many when speaking of a beloved barn.

A two-section or end-to-end Pennsylvania Standard barn complex in southern Pennsylvania. Note the hex signs on the upper level.

created by extending the upper portion of the front wall 4 or more feet. The use of support posts is usually a matter of preference.

It can be confusing to hear descriptors like German barn, bank barn, Pennsylvania German barn, Pennsylvania Standard, cantilevered forebay barn, and even Sweitzer or Swisser (which originated in Canton Schwyz, Switzerland). All describe very nearly the same barn. Colorful hex signs are a 1600s carry-over from Europe. The signs have as much symbolic meaning as people choose to give them. Most are just decorative.

The American pioneer had to act quickly to secure shelter if he and his livestock were to survive, especially during winter months. Many ethnic styles

Monitor-style Virginia log barn with an upper floor and gear sheds.

A well-maintained
Upper Peninsula,
Michigan,
cordwood barn.

of barns were not built immediately because form gave way to function and
for immediate functionality nothing beat a log barn. Most researchers credit
Swedish and Finnish immigrants with bringing the best log-barn designs to
America in about 1630 when America's virgin forests were abundant with
towering straight trees.

Log barns can still be found across the United States, among them the
unique Appalachian overhung-loft barn, Georgia barn, transverse crib barn,
and simple double-crib barn. In 1977, H. Wayne Price, with the group
"Save Our Barns," located 250 log structures remaining in Illinois. Michigan's
Upper Peninsula, Minnesota, and northern Wisconsin have numerous log
barns because the area was settled by large numbers of Swedes and Finns.
The Upper Peninsula and Wisconsin are home to the nation's stovewood
or cordwood barns. The name comes from the fact that the foundation of
these barns was 16- to 20-inch lengths of wood—the same size as firewood.
The wood, second growth after Michigan's forests were cut over to build
cities, was usually cedar, which has high insulation and weather-resisting
properties. The lengths were wrapped in mortar with the butt ends exposed.
Stovewood barns have also been found in Poland and Norway. Because many
were built in the United States during the Great Depression of the 1920s
and 1930s they have also been called "Depression Barns."

An Arkansas barn reveals French influence in its sweeping roofline.

The builder of this and other mid-Michigan barns made them distinctive by their unusual windows, vents and trim.

Intermountain barns evolved around 1890. This one, in Utah, stored hay in the mow, sheltered animals below and allowed snow to slide off low eaves.

The south and southwest are the only part of the country where barns bearing Hispanic influence—built of adobe bricks or *terrones* ("flat clods of earth")—may be found. Plantation barns of sand, lime and oyster shells are found only in the deep south. But for the most part, any style of barn and construction material can be found just about anywhere across the United States. Train travel permitted lumber to be shipped across the country, so, if a person could afford it and trains passed his way, his barn could be built (within reason) with materials from just about anywhere.

Opinions differ as to the age and location of the oldest standing barn in the United States. Few barns remain from the first half of the 1700s. Barn historian Greg Huber cites the dendro-dated Bull Barn in Orange County, New York, as dating to 1726 while one of the oldest, according to Jon Radojkovic in *Barn Building*, is the Jones Log Barn in Pennsylvania, built *c.* 1730. Barn enthusiasts have compiled a list of Dutch-American, English-American, cantilevered forebay barns and swing-beam barns believed to be pre-1780s. In many cases age can be approximated based on evidence of the type of tools used to prepare and fit timbers. Midwestern and southern barns may date as far back as the 1830s. Barns in the far west date from the late nineteenth century. Many barns represent multiple time periods as they have been added onto over several decades.

As farm communities grew, so did the scale and sophistication of their barns. One can still find areas where the ethnicity of the community can be seen in its barns. It is a delight for barn lovers to also make note of how builders often left their mark as a structural enhancement or artistic feature.

The New England region is known for its "connected" or "continuous" barns. The human and animal dwellings were connected, in a line or an L-shape as the "big house, little house, backhouse, barn" immortalized in the old nursery rhyme. This made it easy to pass from one building to another without enduring winter's chill, and in the 1600s and 1700s when settlers were in conflict with Native Americans, to use the connected buildings as a fortress. But they were also exceedingly vulnerable to fire and for a time in the 1600s were banned. Most connected barns in twenty-first century America have been converted to new uses. Still, discussions continue about

New Hampshire connected "big house, little house, backhouse, barn." The barn dates to 1885.

Above: America has extraordinary barns with between five and twenty sides. This two-story limestone beauty was built in Iowa in 1996.

Right: The rebuilding of George Washington's sixteen-sided barn in the mid-1990s.

Below: This concrete barn in northern Indiana is a favorite of photographers.

One of the many types of barn found in Ohio. Note slate roof on main 1883 barn.

their advantages for proximity to valuable livestock, disadvantages in terms of fire risk and insurance rates, and ways to redesign to greatest advantage.

According to Eric Sloane in *An Age of Barns*, round barns were America's first "modern architecture." The circle has spiritual significance, perhaps none more powerfully than its representation of the continuity of faith and life. These barns, along with hexagonal, octagonal, pentagonal, and even decahexagonal (sixteen-sided) and rare oval barns can be found throughout the United States. The greatest number of sides found is twenty. Promoted as being cheaper to build in terms of lumber, they were costlier in labor because it took more skill to build a round barn and if greater than 60 feet in diameter, interior roof supports were needed. Some feature a center silo. Most have a haymow.

The nation's most famous round barn belonged to its first president, George Washington, on Dogue Run Farm, Virginia, now known as Mount Vernon.

A southern rack-sided livestock barn.

15

Top:
"Preservation Virginia" is documenting the state's log tobacco barns.

Middle:
A Kentucky tobacco barn features side ventilation with at least two interior levels for drying tobacco.

Bottom:
This Dutch slice hip-roofed North Carolina barn was probably also used for drying tobacco. It is ventilated at the eaves.

Though more accurately a sixteen-sided barn, Washington designed it himself and had it built by slaves between 1792 and 1794. It was two stories high, 52 feet in diameter of brick and yellow pine, with a cypress-shingled roof. The barn was rebuilt in the mid-1990s.

In *A Field Guide to North American Barns & Other Farm Structures*, Noble and Cleek state that at least twenty major ethnic groups and maybe another twenty lesser-known groups influenced American barn-building. The Irish and Scottish contributed an outstanding knowledge of stone masonry that turned ordinary foundations into works of art. The French are credited with distinctive framing methods; Italians with the addition of masonry pillars.

As noted, many factors besides ethnicity must be taken into account when examining and drawing conclusions about American barns. High on the list are available resources, topography, climate, and intended purpose. Some types are seen in certain regions more than in others. In Ohio, for example— according to Ric Beck with the Friends of Ohio Barns—there are crib log barns in the south-central area, swing-beam barns in the southwest, and English ground barns and Pennsylvania forebays in the northeast. He believes Ohio has a greater variety of barns than any other state, though barn admirers from other states may disagree.

In his book, *Barns*, John Michael Vlach divides the United States into nine regions and provides photographs of the predominant type of barn found in each. A barn built where there was plenty of virgin hardwood and fieldstone would have a different personality than one built where limestone or adobe was in abundance. A barn for cattle may be different than one for sheep. A barn exposed to winds sweeping across a dry prairie requires different construction than one subjected to heavy wet snow. Even for barns serving the same purpose, a tobacco barn in Kentucky looks different from one in Virginia or North Carolina. Yet, it can be a challenge to identify a barn's

Built of glacial granite and pine, this 1888 Montana barn was built by carpenters and stonemasons brought to the States from Italy.

17

Above: The farm with the white buildings (left) was photographed in Wisconsin in 1964 and the other (right) in Pennsylvania in 1972. Different style main barns, yet both used for dairy cattle.

Middle: Joseph Battell had this barn built in 1878 at a cost of $10,000 for prized Morgan horses. The barn is part of the University of Vermont where fine Morgan horses continue to be bred and raised.

Bottom: This castle-like barn in Michigan's famous Sleeping Bear Dunes National Lakeshore was built by immigrant D. H. Day, businessman and farmer. The barns was built in the 1880s for dairy cattle.

Top:
Many barns
have mice inside
but this barn's
resident, similar
to Mickey Mouse
of Walt Disney
fame, greets air
travelers from
the roof as they
pass overhead!

Middle:
This Ohio
bicentennial
mural graces a barn
that was part of a
county-run home
for the poor.

Bottom:
An Ohio barn
proudly states
its owner's
convictions.

The interior of the Breeden Barn, Alaska, clearly showing its Shawver truss design.

location from only an image, due to country-wide migration of people, materials and ingenuity.

Additionally, cultural or religious values must be considered. The Amish and Mennonite communities avoid ornamentation and have strictly functional barns while barns on upscale estates, university campuses or those owned by gentleman farmers or ranchers may be architectural showplaces.

In America, it is common to find the name of the owner and date the farm was purchased or founded, painted on the barn or shingled into the roof. Images of animals and farm equipment are occasionally designed into shingles as well. Murals, quilt patterns, wreaths, seasonal lighting displays, advertisements, and religious or political messages are eye-catching decoration on a barn. One of the most famous advertisements —"Chew Mail Pouch Tobacco Treat Yourself to the Best"—was painted on more than 15,000 barns by the late Harley E. Warrick. Another advertisement encouraged travelers to "See Rock City" in Chattanooga, Tennessee. To honor the state of Ohio's bicentennial (1803–2003), special logos were painted on eighty-eight barns over five years by artist Scott Hagan and documented in the book *Bicentennial Barns,* by Christina Wilkinson.

Historians disagree on whether adaptations occurred in ethnic designs because virgin timber became less available or as people came up with ways to save money or gain space. For these reasons, it has become difficult to easily associate a style of barns with a single ethnic group; however the arrangement and types of farm buildings may assist in pinpointing ethnicity.

John L. Shawver, an architect and builder in Bellefontaine, Ohio, in the late nineteenth century, is credited with a barn design utilizing laminated dimensional lumber in place of solid posts and beams. The Shawver truss or balloon-frame design was said to reduce costs as it required less lumber and hand labor, being constructed from presawn boards 2 inches thick and 4–8 inches wide and of predetermined length and nails, rather than heavy large timbers, handcrafted and fitted by skilled workmen. The design also allowed for wider, uninterrupted spans, thereby increasing storage space. A new means of barn-building had begun.

Over the years, barn historians have identified more than fifty styles of barns. American barns are often described by adjectives that capture one or more terms associated with ethnicity such as a Swedish barn; design (cantilevered); region (Appalachian Meadow); state (Pennsylvania); use (tobacco); and building materials (stone). A barn may also be referred to just by a person's name (Smith Barn). In twenty-first-century America, as barns are being moved and reconstructed, accurate descriptors become less likely, heightening the tremendous importance of documenting the barn's life story in facts and photographs.

If any farm or ranch structure can reluctantly be called American, it is the pole building. Built of dimensional lumber, the building is set on narrow posts topped by a metal gable roof with or without metal or fabric sides called "barn curtains." Unlike its traditional predecessor it goes up quickly, requires few construction skills, and is not built for longevity, a dramatic statement that America is a nation on the move, ever in the midst of change.

An American farm of the twenty-first century is likely to be an eclectic mix of structures. Here, one can find a hoop-frame, a metal pole building, and a traditional barn.

THE HEART OF
EVERY FARM

ANY HOPE of future prosperity for America's homesteaders depended on livestock and crops. It was imperative that animals be well protected— usually an ox or horse, a cow, and a few chickens. If a homesteading family used scant resources to build a house while not providing shelter for the animals, all were unlikely to survive. This inspired the expression, "A barn can build a house, but a house cannot build a barn." The barn could be shared with the animals until the family's situation stabilized. The smell of the animals could be overlooked for the benefit of their warmth, milk, and eggs, and their waste could be used to enrich the soil for growing crops and gardens. Eventually a house could be built, and later a bigger barn.

The concept of housebarns (*einhaus* in the Netherlands and *bauernhaus* in Germany), did not readily transfer to America as a permanent arrangement, except in New England. Occasionally, house barns or connected barns are found in other parts of the United States.

Grey Osterud, author of *Putting the Barn Before the House: Women and Family Farming in Early Twentieth-Century New York,* shares an account of a Ukranian immigrant who moved with her husband to a farm in Maine in 1932. The house was unfit to live in and while the husband wanted to build a new one, he said he had better build the barn first because, "If we build the barn, the cows will build the house."

He was not the first immigrant to grasp the significance of a good barn. John DeCrevecoeur, author of *Letters from an American Farmer, c.* 1770, wrote that farmers believed their barns needed to be superior to their dwelling: "Many don't care how they are lodged, provided that they have a good barn and barn yard."

In all likelihood, more than one farm woman reached the limit of her patience when her husband wanted to improve the barn while she made do with a less-than-desirable house. The expression, "You can tell who wears the pants," was often associated with comparing the condition of the house to that of the barn. A nicer house might be taken to show that the wife was in control. As women's ability to manage entire farm operations has been

This Upper Peninsula, Michigan, log barn dates to the mid-1800s and its addition to the early 1900s.

The log barn in the center background was likely the first structure built on this 1800s Midwest farm, belonging to the author's ancestors.

recognized, the expression has less meaning. Women have always known that the barn is the heart of the farm and must be maintained. Some people working in barn preservation believe that women more than men are the motivating force behind saving barns as they advocate for their historic, aesthetic, and practical value.

The movement of immigrants throughout America was bolstered by the merging of the Union Pacific and Central Pacific railroads in May 1869. This opened a main line on which goods could be shipped coast to coast, though for many the prairie schooner or Conestoga wagon was still the only means of travel. As soil and forests were depleted in one part of the vast continent,

These old "connected" barns in Chilili, New Mexico, are built of saddle-notched logs.

JERRY R. DAVIS
2012

people sought out new terrain. Others, lured by talk of money to be made during the Gold Rush of the mid-nineteenth century, headed west.

Some immigrants chose to settle on land that most resembled what they had known in "the Old Country." The rolling hills of Pennsylvania drew German and Swiss farmers in droves. Swedes and Finns headed to Minnesota and Michigan. Populations in the south and southwest already reflected the influence of Spanish-speaking immigrants who introduced barn designs which—according to John Michael Vlach—originated on the Iberian Peninsula. Settlers in the south and southwest followed waterways, building adobe and log homes with courtyard layouts like mini-fortresses.

Once a family made it through the first difficult years and could replace an earthen or log shelter with something more substantial, America's marvelous barns began to rise on the horizon. America was a land of farmers. Tradition, if not necessity, held that at some point offspring would take over the family farm. From generation to generation, there would always be a "home place" where a living could be made and a family could be raised.

A barn rises on the North Dakota landscape in 1915.

This work of art was built on the Shepp Ranch near Alma, Kansas, in 1905.

A senior member of the Amish community, Holmes County, Ohio, demonstrates, inside a simulated barn frame, how a hay sling lifts and moves loose hay for storage.

The barn and house were built solidly with forever in mind, accounting for why some still stand a century or more later.

Many early statesmen, including Thomas Jefferson and Benjamin Franklin, believed farming would forever be the national endeavor. As Eric Sloane wrote in *An Age of Barns*, there was a time in the life of the nation when a man might have another profession, but he was also a farmer because he had to be.

In 1796, a policy was established allowing land speculators to buy 620-acre tracts for two dollars an acre. Over time this policy was revised until in 1862 the Homestead Act was created, giving 160 acres of free land to settlers. With 270 million acres available, the excitement was palpable. Three requirements had to be met. Settlers must be twenty-one years of age, the head of a household, and able to pay an eighteen-dollar filing fee. After that, the homesteader's task was to build a house and a barn if possible and live on the land for five years in order to claim full title.

Land was plentiful but the population was still small. Word went back to the Old Country, whether it was Europe or South America, to come to America, and after the Civil War, more immigrants arrived. Like those before them, they brought a fine knowledge of barn-building. Improvements in the technology of sawing lumber in this period are mirrored in changes in barn construction.

At the start of the nineteenth century roughly 80 percent of the population lived on family farms (worked by and sustaining a family). President Thomas Jefferson's system of creating numbered sections of land, with 640 acres per section, documented farms within each section and made it easier to lay out corresponding roadways.

Tobacco and cotton were the nation's primary agricultural products on much of the east coast but as farmers migrated they learned what worked best in differing terrains, soil conditions, and climates. Sprawling beef cattle ranches grew from Texas to the Dakota Territory of Wyoming, Colorado, Nebraska, and Kansas, where initially fertile grasslands sustained the herds. There, as grasslands were overgrazed, leading to the need for hay, barns with long, sweeping roofs known as prairie barns were built. Often these had a hay hood to enable loose hay to be lifted from a wagon using a hayfork or system of wooden slats and rope, taken in through an upper door, moved using a hay track and carrier mounted to the ridge of the barn, and stored inside.

Similar hay-carrier systems, designed by William Louden in 1867, were used in the Midwest. But there, the gambrel-roofed barn came into vogue, using balloon framing with sawn dimensional lumber. This double-pitched,

Top: A classic prairie barn, "Kelly Creek Ranch No. 1," in New Pine Creek, Oregon.

Inset: Several publications, such as this one c. 1920, encouraged farmers to put down roots, literally and figuratively.

27

A gothic, arched, round, or rainbow-roofed barn in northern Ohio.

Early wooden and concrete silos remain on this Wisconsin farm.

symmetrical roof allowed for the upper portion of the barn to efficiently store larger amounts of hay or straw bedding. The structural load could be better distributed and the amount of wood needed to build a barn decreased. The arrival of mechanical balers and elevators in the 1940s turned hay carriers into

dusty chandeliers except on Amish farms. String- or wire-bound rectangular bales could be placed on elevators and stacked in mows by the hundreds.

Another type of roof that came onto the scene in about 1915 using dimensional lumber was the gothic or rainbow roof. Like the gambrel, it allowed for maximum mow storage, but was also praised for its ability to withstand wind by allowing air to move up and over the roof without resistance.

In addition to the gambrel roof, the Midwest—because of its suitability for the dairy industry—became recognized for its dairy barns and silos (used to store silage, a fermented feed made from chopped corn). Land-grant colleges and universities, founded through the Morrill Act of 1862 to specialize in agriculture and the mechanical arts, designed barns, silos, and complementary structures. The first documented wooden upright silo was built in Illinois in 1873 but by the 1900s ever taller silos were being built of stone and later block, tile, or steel. As herd size increased, barns and silos got bigger and government regulations governing the sanitary production of wholesome milk were enacted to protect public health.

Beginning in about 1910, in order to sell milk at the highest quality level and at better prices, farmers had to milk cows on washable concrete floors. Milk had to be stored in a temperature-controlled area separate from the cattle. Block "milk houses" were attached to the barn, replacing storage in small stone buildings built over creeks or into the ground to keep milk cold.

Above left:
Compact square bales fill the mow of this Midwest barn.

Above right:
A block milk house is neatly attached to a Michigan gambrel-roof barn.

This potato barn is well grounded in Connecticut.

Gutters behind cows captured manure and conveyor systems carried it out of the barn. The names "Jamesway" and "De Laval" became well-known: Jamesway, for stanchions, ventilators, and manure-handling systems; De Laval for milking equipment and cream separators. By 1950 the name "Harvestor" would be associated with tall, blue silos. Farming was greatly aided by the Rural Electrification Act of 1936 which increased farm productivity and relieved aching backs.

Before the construction of silos, corn was stored in a crib barn or corn crib, a well-ventilated but also very rodent-ridden wood-frame structure. Crib barns were built in many parts of the country but are still seen most frequently in the south and southeast. Potato farming, which began in the early eighteenth century and was at its peak by the early twentieth century, primarily in the east coast Long Island region, led to the design of curious potato barns which look as if a traditional barn has sunk into the ground to its eaves. These barns store potatoes below ground at even, cool temperatures.

Thus, no matter in what part of the United States an early settler or a modern-day farmer or rancher might reside, at the heart of every enterprise was its barn. Many an oral or a written history of a farm uses the barn as the benchmark for time and important events: "It happened the year after the barn was built," or, "That was the summer we added on to the barn." The barn was where the work day began and often ended. People came together to build the barn and when the last peg or nail was driven, a dance might be held in the brand new structure. When a community had no church, services might be held in a barn until one could be built. For these reasons and more, it is difficult to understand why barns have too often gotten short-shrift from the nation they built. If the Bald Eagle is America's national bird, many believe the barn should be its national building.

A familiar scene from the early 1960s—a barn at the heart of a productive American farm, this was the Michigan farm on which the author was raised.

FORM, FIT, AND FUNCTION

WHETHER ERECTING a log barn or a timber-frame barn, builders need four things: good timber, good tools, good sense, and good neighbors. These qualities were especially essential when construction was more dependent on hand labor, and the margin for error was virtually non-existent. The preparatory work required long hours of back-straining effort. Mistakes were unbearable. A towering tree, felled and hewn into a massive beam, then cured for a year, could not be replaced as easily as can dimensional lumber from the local lumber yard. If many men are working together with muscle and might, ropes and pike poles, to raise a section of barn frame (known as a bent), no one wants to hear "Oops, I measured wrong" when thousands of pounds of timber are nearly in place.

For those familiar with the architecture of timber-frame barns, terms like sills, purlins, girts, queen posts, braces, king posts, rafters, bays, and bents are just a few of the words in their working vocabulary. Words like mortise and tenon and peg are spoken with reverence because they refer to a frame built without nails with tremendous attention paid to every detail. The story pole, or measuring staff, is as important to a barn-builder as a compass is to a ship's captain because on it is marked every essential measurement.

The building of a timber-frame barn begins with the aging of the timbers, as freshly cut wood is wet, heavy, and apt to split, warp, and twist. If a barn is built entirely by hand labor, a variety of tools are used to hew the logs square, measure lengths to ensure proper fit, and cut an opening into one (mortise) to receive a protruding piece from another (tenon). Meanwhile, other members of the frame are also being made so that, like pieces of a puzzle, every piece fits and bears its weight appropriately. Wooden pegs hold the frame together through holes (drilled with an auger) into the mortise and tenon joinery at corners, braces, and all other points where parts of the frame come together.

The same need for attention to detail was true for the construction of log barns, which were built using one of two styles: an "even tier" in which logs were laid evenly all the way around by being cut to fit into a corner post,

Opposite: Looks can be deceiving. This barn, built by Bob Hetz, Battle Creek, Michigan, is just 23 inches high by 15 wide and 26 long, patterned after barns of his youth. This miniature features stalls for animals, a ladder to a small loft and above it, yet another loft. The barn always stirs, "I remember when...." stories from viewers.

or "alternating tier." For the latter design, the logs were notched, using cuts such as square or round, v-notch or saddle notch, dovetail or half-dovetail. They were then fitted together. The roof was usually shingled with slabs salvaged from the tree's outer layers and bark, 3 to 4 feet long and horizontally overlapped by about 50 percent. The space between the logs was filled with "chinking": a mixture made from mud, straw, grass, or even cattle manure. This kept the cold out and warmth in. Upper logs were left unchinked to provide air flow as it was believed an air-tight barn was unhealthy for animals. A similar, but controversial, sentiment exists two centuries later with regard to pole buildings. Some people have attributed joint stiffness and lung infections in animals and rusting in machinery to the lack of air movement and condensation inside metal buildings. Refinements have been made and pole, or prefabricated buildings, are now used throughout the United States.

Controversy also exists over whether it is cheaper to put up a pole building than to repair a traditional timber-frame barn. There is no one answer, as there are many considerations, such as the condition of the existing barn and the intended use. Tax implications are high on the list since new construction is generally taxed higher than are repairs to an existing building. Many agree that a traditional barn is a more durable and infinitely more

Amish barn builders work together to raise a bent.

Above:
The hand-hewn plate (horizontal beam at right) of this century-old barn stretches more than 40 feet. Rough-sawn roof boards from virgin timber are more than 18 inches wide.

Left:
Attention to detail shows in a pegged post and the braces of a 1900 timber-frame barn being dismantled for reconstruction at a new location.

attractive structure. As traditional barns are now being re-sided in steel, another American adaptation is being created.

Whereas the first log barns were essentially one box-like structure, later log or log crib barns might be four separate units with a second story above and an aisleway through the center, allowing for a wagon to completely pass through the barn side-to-side or end-to-end.

More early log barns and log homes still exist, hidden under boards, tar paper, or even metal or vinyl siding. For some, this was a matter of increasing the utility of the structure. For others, it was a means of dressing up an old barn to make it fit for a changing society which tended to associate log structures with being primitive or crude.

Log structures are still being built, though almost exclusively for display at historic sites, to teach the craft, or to become prestigious homes and lodges. Pioneers, who were eager to move out of a log structure, would shake their heads in wonderment.

Barn-building changed when builders had access to sawmills. The earliest known water-powered mill was built in Maine in 1623 but not until the early 1800s in the Midwest and further west. Steam later replaced waterpower and "up and down" saws were replaced by circular blades as early as 1838. This means that marks on posts and beams can reveal the approximate age of the barn as it can be seen whether the wood was processed in a sawmill and if so, what kind of blade was used. Other advancements came with

This log cabin was quite impressive in its day— the mid-1800s.

Craftsmanship has helped this northern log barn to remain in use more than one hundred and fifty years after it was built.

the invention of planing and nail-making machines in the late 1700s. By the mid-twentieth century, barn builders had the benefit of tractors, trucks, hoists, and cranes to assist with the heavy and dangerous lifting. Dimensional and laminated lumber had taken the place of most solid timber-frame construction.

When done by hand, the foundation of the barn is built and mortises are cut into the sill or base supporting timbers. The bents are then prepared on the ground and positioned into place using a series of carefully coordinated steps, involving lifting, pushing with pike poles, and bracing with planks to take the full weight off the crew, while tapping the bases of the bent with mauls until each tenon lines up with and settles into the correct mortise in the sill. A gin pole may be used to aid the process as well. To place beams at the top of a frame, scaffolding is built and each beam is raised using muscle, ropes, and pulleys. Many injuries and fatalities have occurred in the process of building a traditional barn.

Teamwork is also essential when moving a barn. Barns have been moved for as long as they have been built, initially with the help of horses or oxen. But it is possible to move a barn if enough man- and womanpower can be garnered as proven in Bruno, Nebraska in July 1988 when 344 people took

In the early hours of August 26, 2007, the Breeden Barn was moved from Matanuska to the grounds of the Museum of Alaska Transportation and Industry, Wasilla. The barn is actually two c. 1930s barns, one of which had already been moved once to be joined to the other.

up position around a metal frame affixed to a 17,000-pound barn and in unison, lifted, walked, and moved it a short distance to higher ground. Each person bore about 56 pounds of barn and frame weight. The video of this feat has been viewed online thousands of times.

Another type of barn raising that took place in America until about 1936 was the building of "kit barns." Several companies already producing "kit houses," by the late nineteenth century, expanded their line of pre-designed, precut, prepackaged homes to include barns and other farm buildings. A customer could choose from a variety of roof styles and could even purchase a round or polygonal barn. At its peak in 1919, Sears, Roebuck and Company offered twenty-six different models. The barns arrived with everything packaged and accounted for, right down to nails, shingles, and paint. Agricultural colleges and companies also sold a variety of barn, outbuilding and silo designs. The University of Illinois, for example, in 1910 published a bulletin, "The Economy of the Round Dairy Barn," and in 1918 updated and republished it as "The Round Barn."

Most barn raisings in twenty-first-century America, unless done the old-fashioned way, lack creativity and personality. Prefabricated metal buildings have come a long way as ventilators, cupolas, and ornate doors and windows have been added. But watching a stick-frame structure quickly fastened together with power equipment with screwed-on metal siding and roofing cannot take the place of the intimate relationship with timber, tools, and teamwork that was required to build the kind of barn that shaped America.

Above:
The "Sylvania" was a 210-foot kit barn with a 14-foot-wide riding ring inside its outer walls. Sold by Sears, Roebuck and Company, this model was built on Meadowfarm in Orange, Virginia as a boarding stable.

Opposite:
Affectionately called "Old Girl" by its owner, this kit barn stands proudly in southwest Michigan.

BARNS IN DECLINE

TIMBER-FRAME BARN construction in the United States continued into the early twentieth century; framing with dimensional lumber until roughly the 1950s. In 1935, the peak year for family farms in America, there were 6.8 million, with most having at least one barn. After World War II, the average farm doubled in size from 300 to 600 acres. The consolidation of farms was beginning and with it the beginning of the end for traditional American barns.

In 1798, tax records identified not just how many barns there were in one part of Pennsylvania, but how many were log, timber-frame, stone, or stone and log. Yet, more than two centuries later, despite sophisticated systems for gathering and analyzing data, records compiled about barns are paltry. Only nudging from the National Barn Alliance—a nonprofit group of barn enthusiasts—persuaded the United States Department of Agriculture (USDA) to ask, in its 2007 agricultural survey, whether farmers and ranchers owned a pre-1960 barn. The very organization overseeing farming had not intended to document the fate of the structure that had once been the heart of every farm.

The USDA's 2007 census reported just 664,264 pre-1960 barns on farms and ranches throughout the entire fifty states though it did not count multiple barns on the same farm or ranch, operations earning less than $1,000 per year, or barns that were no longer part of a farm. Texas reported the most with about 51,000, followed by Missouri at 36,000 and Wisconsin at 35,000.

The causes for the death of traditional barns in America are many. Early barns were lost during the Revolutionary War, battles between Native Americans and settlers known as the French and Indian War, the Indian Wars, the Civil War, and conflicts between settlers.

Change also came as industrialization—which had begun prior to the Civil War—meant that taking over the family farm was not what some of the sons and daughters of post-Civil War America had in mind. In fact, by 1860, a year before the outbreak of the Civil War, the nation was already so industrialized that the value of manufactured goods was five times greater

Opposite:
Back-breaking labor went into the building of a now-abandoned, century-old barn in Michigan's Upper Peninsula.

41

April 14, 1935 is remembered as "Black Sunday," when western topsoil swept eastward with such force, it reached the Atlantic Ocean.

APPROACHING DUST STORM IN MIDDLE WEST.

than that of all the crops combined. By the late nineteenth century all open land was spoken for.

Young people began to leave the farm for the allure of city life and careers in business and industry. Terms like "hicks from the sticks" and "plow jockey" would be used to demean someone from a rural area. To ask, "Were you born in a barn?" was to suggest you had no social graces.

For those who remained in farming, industry was creeping into their vocation as well. A man by the name of John Deere had perfected a plow in the late 1830s and Cyrus McCormick invented a machine to harvest grain.

The author's grandfather, shows off his first tractor, a McCormick Deering Farmall, in the 1920s.

Left and bottom:
Some traditional
barns are able
to store round
bales but for large
farms, metal sheds
are more efficient.

Introduced in the late nineteenth century, tractors changed farming forever
Although the capacity to work the land was now measured in horsepower, it
did not involve the labor of a single horse.

Progress would prove to be both the boon and bane of traditional barns.
As farmers used machinery to work more acreage and clear more land,
increased productivity might mean they needed more barns ("boon"). But
these inventions also initiated the "bane" phase as they helped to deplete
hundreds of thousands of acres of the nation's forests and soil. In the
Great Plains states, grassland was plowed deeply without rotating crops or
replanting trees to hold the soil. Drought brought disaster. History records
the financial ruin of many families brought on by "The Dust Bowl" of the
1930s and the Great Depression with its stock market crash. Farms across
the country were abandoned.

After World War II, farms began to specialize and consolidate. Farming
methods changed almost overnight with everything getting bigger except
the traditional barn, which was becoming obsolete. A twenty-first-century

farmer can operate a "CAFO" (concentrated animal feedlot operation) where hundreds of animals are confined to long, large metal buildings where they produce milk, eggs, or are fattened for slaughter. A farmer can work thousands of acres using mammoth, computer-aided machinery. Square bales of hay or straw weighing 50 pounds have been replaced by round bales weighing several hundred pounds making most traditional barns impractical for storage.

It is hard to argue, in some cases, with the farmer who says he has no need for an old barn as a place to milk cows. His grandfather might have milked Flossie, Bessie, and a few bovine companions by hand morning and night in individual stalls. His father's herd likely topped out at sixty to a hundred ear-tagged cows milked by machine twice a day in two rows of stanchions. Today's farmer may have hundreds to thousands of radio-frequency-tagged, computer-cataloged cattle being milked three to six times a day on rotating platforms or by laser-guided robots in mechanized chambers. The Hawaiian Island of Oahu closed its last dairy operation in the early 2000s. Traditional barns, never plentiful on the Islands, have become even more scarce, lost to a changing economy and rapid development.

Dairy cattle move and eat freely in this large, open pole-frame metal structure.

This weary barn
will soon fall
victim to a
strong wind
or heavy snow.

Other changes affecting the well-being of America's barns occur continuously at the policy level as farmers, ranches, agricultural organizations, policymakers, and corporations wrangle over crop insurance; price supports; subsidies; land values; international trade; the use and labeling of genetically modified organisms (GMOs); regulation of pesticides, herbicides, fungicides, and fertilizers; community-supported agriculture (CSA), and other highly charged issues. Countless farmers have suffered catastrophic losses by borrowing too much money when land values were high or by putting too much emphasis on a particular crop or animal only to see prices bottom out.

These fabric
structures have
many uses but do
they really deserve
to be called barns?

45

Tennessee barns stand empty as an elite subdivision consumes their farm and a nearby mountain.

Surrounded by box stores and fast food outlets, the barn was the last to go, but in this case Walmart Corporation paid to have it dismantled and its frame reused to build a barn used for youth programs 60 miles away.

So what of the traditional barn? In the best of all worlds it has found a new use on the farm as a workshop, starter barn for young animals, or another agricultural purpose. The mow may have been removed and frame re-trussed to accommodate larger equipment. But in the worst-case scenario, it has been hastily destroyed and replaced by a metal or polyethylene structure, or is dying slowly, struggling to stand straight like an aging veteran in a Fourth of July parade.

This sad Ohio barn needed a friend a long time ago. What stories might it tell of its best days and once valuable life as the heart of a farm?

Bottom:
Rain through roofs and vines that strangle, hold moisture, break siding, and add weight, spell death for traditional barns.

But it is not change alone in agriculture that has affected the health of America's traditional barns. It is America's propensity toward haste and waste. The construction of super highways has bled the hearts of America's farms. The rush to plant suburbia where crops once flourished—along with copy-cat strip-malls, fast-food restaurants, box stores, and acres of asphalt— has accounted for the sudden death of countless farms and barns.

Barns are lost to nature's wrath—lightning strikes, tornadoes, high winds, flooding, and heavy snowfall—though Benjamin Franklin's invention

Several barns on the campus of Michigan State University (formerly Michigan State College) no longer exist. Some continue as barns; others have been given adaptive new uses.

Only one of these barns for cattle and hogs remains on the grounds of the North Dakota State Penitentiary in Bismarck. They were built c. 1930 so that inmates could raise their own food. The remaining barn is used for storage.

of the lightning rod in 1749, which transfers electrical energy by cable and rod to the ground, has saved countless structures. Barns are also lost to spontaneous combustion caused by fermenting hay as well as insect and rodent infestation, and—in 2012 probably more than at any time in the nation's history—to wildfires that ravaged millions of acres and countless homes and barns, primarily in the west.

"Mother Nature" cannot be controlled (though people continue to try). It is the willful effects of human carelessness and neglect that are destroying more American barns: tree roots allowed to grow into foundations, branches

clawing at shingles, vines cracking siding and trapping moisture against wood and under eaves, water seeping through roofs, walls, and into frames and foundations, and fires caused by carelessness. Each and every one of these death blows is preventable.

Yet the reasons for the death of America's traditional barns don't even stop there. Coal exploration and mining, oil and gas acquisition, the redirection of waterways and the construction of dams have caused the destruction of barns. Barns were once a part of how people confined to mental institutions and prisons, or living on "poor farms," helped to provide for their own care by tending animals and crops while getting exercise, acquiring skills, and renewing self-respect. Changes in government regulations determined such labor inappropriate and as a result many unusually large, well-constructed barns were destroyed. As motivations and methods have changed, land-grant agricultural colleges established under the Morrill Act have demolished many of their own masterpiece barns. Some have wisely moved, donated, or converted other barns to new uses.

Most people in twenty-first-century America have no experience with barns. Even for those who consider themselves to be experts in vernacular architecture, the only way to identify a structure is to examine its original footprint and form. Adaptations have altered authenticity. While it is currently still possible to recognize the ethnicity of a region by a predominant type of barn found there, even that is changing as barns are being dismantled in one part of the country and rebuilt in another.

This and other Midwest barns have been dismantled and taken to Louisiana, their valuable frames used in upscale housing. Some have survived as barns.

WHEN EVERYTHING OLD IS NEW AGAIN

M ORE of America's traditional barns are being lost than are being saved. In spite of this, there is reason for optimism which comes from the many sensible reasons for saving them. High on the list is the sheer practicality of reusing such solid structures, particularly irreplaceable virgin-timber frame barns. There is also nostalgia, historical importance, the appeal of owning something unique, amazing open space, and the trend back to a healthier relationship with the earth for which a venerable wood-frame barn is emblematic. It comes from the fact that barn-preservation organizations throughout the United States could appropriately adopt a line from an old song: "Don't throw the past away, you might need it again some rainy day... when everything old is new again."

The irony in these words is based in fact. When America was young many people working the land were eager to be free of their old barn, particularly if they had lived in it. A young person could hardly wait to get away from fields and dirt-smudged clothing. But in twenty-first-century America, people are transforming old barns into extraordinary homes, exchanging city commutes and business suits for farm lanes and blue jeans. New entrepreneurs are choosing to use the land sustainably and raise livestock humanely. Agricultural colleges are seeing an upward spike in enrollment. Farm markets are thriving, food cooperatives are blooming, and organic growers, battered by the criticisms of corporate agriculture, are organizing to protect their rights as producers. Hoop-houses sprout near traditional barns.

While some corporations and "big agriculture" fight these trends, others embrace them. One of the most poignant examples of this is the 2011 Chipotle commercial, "Back to the Start," based on the song, "The Scientist." An animation begins with a happy farmer, contented animals, and bright red barns, then transitions to cold metal warehouses where sad animals are processed into cubes. The farmer is miserable because as the song says, "Science and progress don't speak as loud as my heart." He chooses to return to a life with happy animals and red barns at its heart. The Chipotle animation

Opposite: Green Acres, a 1940s dairy barn in Eden Prairie, Minnesota, has become a popular enchanting event center complete with its own wine cellar silo.

The DeBacker Family Dairy retail store in Daggett, Michigan, sells an array of fresh farm produce just a short distance from the family's cattle and crops.

is one example of how images of barns are increasingly being used to illustrate values of wholesome living, honest labor, trustworthiness, and quality.

Omega Farms is a 4,000-acre Angus cattle farm in Williamston, Michigan, created through the consolidation of several farms in the 1960s. In 2008 they began to restore the barns on those farms. Owners say thousands of visitors each year are drawn to the eighteen restored traditional barns. This educates people about their importance, and creates marketing appeal for the enterprise, which emphasizes its stewardship of the land, livestock, and wildlife.

This barn home allows the beauty of its frame and natural wood to create a place of warmth and welcome.

This home's previous life as a gambrel-roofed barn is evident. The silo serves as a stairwell with a circular staircase suspended from cables. The entire third level is an office with an extraordinary view.

Even the country-music industry has taken respect for farming to a higher level. If listeners are to make a judgment about people from rural settings or farm life based on the lyrics, they may conclude that there are no better people and no better way to live, especially if you have a barn and a big green tractor.

The desire to have a barn in twenty-first-century America is not entirely about returning to farming as a livelihood. In some cases visitors are the cash crop, as they pay to experience farm chores firsthand. Part of a growing interest in "agri-tourism," these opportunities provide the financial means for people to use and maintain their barns. Increasingly popular are "breakfast on the farm" events allowing the public a firsthand look at and taste of today's agriculture.

A large Millersburg, Ohio barn has become the Barn Inn, a popular bed and breakfast. (Note quilt mural.)

This weathered barn serves as the offices for the Mast Farm Inn, Valle Crucis, North Carolina. On the National Register of Historic Places, the farm is steeped in history.

Below and opposite bottom: After life as the stable for horses and wagons used by Sullivan Dairy, a milk delivery business in Battle Creek, Michigan, this 1922 barn stood empty. It was purchased in 2001 by businessmen and transformed into offices.

Farmer-owned retail stores sell freshly made cheese, ice cream, and other produce grown literally within eyesight.

Traditional barns are also at the heart of many nature centers, historic villages, county and state fairgrounds, eco-villages, holistic healing retreats, and training centers where people can learn traditional and sustainable farming methods and building construction. Conscientious developers have creatively incorporated farm structures into tracts for new housing, giving them new life as community centers, offices or part of historic parks. Some land-grant universities continue to use barns creatively. Some remain in use as working barns, while others have been converted to event sites, workshops, classrooms, and storage facilities. As wind turbines rise by the hundreds from America's farm fields, the hope is that income they generate will save the barns they overshadow.

When the Kresge Foundation, Troy, Michigan, bought a farm as the new site for its headquarters it moved a barn there to replace an 1852 barn lost a few years earlier. The barn and original farmstead structures are now part of its office complex as a way to preserve farm history.

As these trends continue, there will be more reasons for those who have traditional barns to keep them in repair. On occasion, realtors are asked about property with a good barn because traditional barns glow with character and their open space promises endless potential as offices, art galleries, retail centers, recording or art studios, museums, antique shops, salons, kennels, restaurants, gathering places, display centers, and bed and breakfasts. Barns are popular as a setting in which to be married, as is readily evidenced by the expanding list of "barn wedding" websites and brides exchanging ideas and recommendations. Where farmland has been converted to golf courses, barns have become clubhouses, restaurants, workshops, or storage centers. But no matter what the new use, the most appealing adaptively reused barns are those that retain as much of the original look and line as possible both internally and externally.

When an Iowa school system wanted to demolish a brick dairy barn on its property, citizens formed "Friends of the Maplenol Barn" to save it. The barn was sold to a church and relocated.

As noted earlier, barns have been moved for as long as they have been built. In one case, five English barns of approximately the same size were moved in the late nineteenth century in Pawlet, Vermont, to become one continuous structure. Depending on the size, location, and condition of the barn, the move to a new location may be done with the barn intact, in sections, or completely disassembled to be rebuilt like a puzzle. Dismantling an old barn and rebuilding it elsewhere gives new meaning to the term "kit barn." Entire businesses have sprung up, specializing in moving barns. In fact, barn-lovers in New York State unhappily say that if you want to see a New York barn, go to Texas. Canadian barns have crossed the border into the United States.

The Manning, Iowa *hausbarn* or *bauernhaus* earns the honor of the oldest barn having been moved the furthest distance. It is a 1660s structure, which in 1999 was donated by a farmer in the Schleswig-Holstein area of Germany to Manning, a community settled by German immigrants. The grand barn has been restored as part of Manning Heritage Park.

The extraordinary 1600s German *bauernhaus* is now at home in Manning, Iowa.

America's virgin forests are nearly gone and with them, wood of the quality and character found in heritage barns. For those who cherish traditional barns, the practice of "harvesting" barns for purposes other than to save other barns, is just one step removed from losing them entirely. Many companies deconstruct barns, sometimes to salvage wood. Admittedly, it is preferable to see great-grandfather's barn live on as mantles, flooring, or tables than to be buried or burned.

In the best of all worlds, a barn remains a working barn. In the worst of all nightmares it is used ostensibly as a fire department "training exercise." The caption under a 2002 newspaper photograph of a large timber-frame barn fully engulfed in flames said, "It was nothing to get upset about. The barn was donated for fire department training." Such callous disregard is wasteful, irreversible, and tragic. Barns are not suited for teaching fire safety. They are built differently than houses and do not contain the same chemical and obstructive hazards.

Educating the public, but most especially barn owners, zoning officials, building inspectors, developers, realtors, insurance agents, firemen, and legislators is the mission of many barn-preservation organizations. In 2012, Historic Barns of Connecticut, a project of the Connecticut Trust for Historic Preservation, conducted a survey of barn organizations in the United States. The project revealed that there were at least eighteen established groups, some founded as early as the mid-1990s, including the National Barn Alliance which encourages collaboration among groups. In addition, the survey identified another seventeen programs getting established. More have formed since the survey.

Some groups are stand-alone registered nonprofit organizations, while others are programs within state historic preservation organizations. They call themselves alliances, coalitions, networks, societies, and most affectionately, "Friends of..." as in the case of the Friends of Ohio Barns or Friends of Minnesota Barns. While most are statewide organizations, others focus on a specific type of barn such the Dutch Barn Preservation Society and the Sweitzer & Log Crib Barn Alliance—alternately known as the International Barn Alliance as it focuses on identifying and preserving these particular barns in the United States and Europe.

The most frequently asked question of barn organizations has to do with the availability of grants. Some make grants and others want to. Grant-making can be a very complicated process and there is great variation among the states on the terms attached to grants: the amount awarded, whether grant dollars must be matched, how the money may be used, what type of work is permitted, whether grants can go to private citizens or are limited to nonprofit groups or municipalities, how accomplishments must be reported, and what measures will assess long-term outcomes. Some restrict

grants to barns already listed on the National Register of Historic Places or their own state historic buildings register. Being listed on the National Register means the barn has been deemed unusually important in its architecture, ownership, or history. Famous architect Frank Lloyd Wright, for example, designed and built a barn as part of his Wisconsin farm, Taliesin, named for a Welsh poet. Other barns were hiding places on the Underground Railroad (the secret network of hiding places for runaway slaves as they sought freedom in the mid-nineteenth century). National Register status does not guarantee that the barn will be preserved; it only elevates its stature. Funds to underwrite these programs come from federal and state grants, foundations, and private citizens. Another incentive to preserve heritage barns is the receipt of tax credits that offset the expense. Only a handful of states offer a tax credit, some up to 25 percent, but again, there are restrictions. In New York for example, the barn must have been built before 1936 and the work cannot materially alter the barn's historic appearance. Other states are working to get barn tax credit legislation passed.

Children eagerly learn how mortise and tenon fit together in a model barn belonging to the National Barn Alliance.

More frequently—particularly given that most barn preservation organizations are solely volunteer-driven—activities include barn surveys, educational workshops, conferences, newsletters, websites, and barn tours. Some organizations' websites are a wealth of information providing ideas for adaptive reuse, barns available for relocation, case studies, survey outcomes, and links to other resources.

Barn surveys attempt to document surviving barns in photos, schematics, and videos, accompanied by as much detail as can be determined. The most successful surveys are those conducted with grant support, professional guidance, and the commitment of devoted volunteers. Some states, rather than sending people out to document the barns, rely on barn owners to self-report. The mantra for anyone passionate about saving America's heritage barns is that the first step in preservation is documentation.

Conferences, workshops, and special events enable people to learn about barn repair, confer with those who specialize in repairing and adapting barns, and access resource materials, such as the National Trust for Historic Preservation's *Using Old Farm Buildings: Adaptations for new agricultural uses*, which is a series of case studies demonstrating how heritage barns of various

Left and bottom: German immigrants Daniel Krause and stonemason Wilhelm Mensenkamp built this 1903 fieldstone barn in Wisconsin. Named for the town of Chase, the Chase Stone Barn Committee has organized to make it an agricultural museum.

kinds have been successfully revamped without losing their historic character. Workshops discuss tax incentives, agri-tourism, the evolution of barns, and encourage barn people to benefit from one another's expertise. Some have scale models of barns to demonstrate the construction of timber-frame barns, and the teamwork needed to raise them.

Another program growing in popularity, not just with barn organizations but with farm-related and tourism associations, are barn tours. Farm tours are not a new concept, having started in the mid-1900s for farmers to learn from one another, and are usually hosted by university extension programs and farm organizations. Focused barn tours in the twenty-first century are more for enjoyment and take a variety of forms in at least twenty-two states. There are narrated and self-guided tours. Scheduled tours usually allow visitors inside many barns with the owner available to answer questions. In 2010, the International Barn Alliance offered a "virtual" barn tour online.

Michigan farmer Robert A. Getzloff chose to keep the family's traditional barn as the heart of his modern dairy operation. The red free-stall metal building (left) shelters cattle while the white family barn (center) is a high-tech milking parlor. Animal feed is stored in the white plastic-wrapped mounds.

Also growing in popularity is the placement of quilt patterns on heritage barns, either painted directly on barn siding or mounted to the barn. These artistic creations may be designed randomly or may relate to historic folk art of the area. Some states produce booklets devoted to the locations and stories of barn quilt blocks in a region, county, or across an entire state. A dozen states feature barn quilts. A book released in 2012—*Barn Quilts and the American Quilt Trail Movement*—looks at this phenomenon with author Suzi Parron concluding that barn quilts have a positive impact on the local economy as they boost tourism and influence farm preservation as people realize that time spent traveling backroads in rural America invites relaxation and renewal. Barn murals also attract attention.

People love barns, especially those they know intimately. When Reiman Publications of Greendale, Wisconsin invited subscribers to its various farm magazines to submit photographs and stories for a book, entries and sentimental stories arrived in the thousands. The result was published in 1996, titled *This Old Barn*.

The National Trust for Historic Preservation's BARN AGAIN!© program—which ran 1987–2009 and gave awards 1998–2009, in partnership with *Successful Farming* magazine—drew nationwide attention to the significance of America's heritage barns. The program annually recognized barns, nominated on a competitive basis, which had been rehabilitated for new farming uses; provided *Using Old Farm Buildings* and a series of topical supplements to farmers across the nation to help them correctly adapt old barns for new uses; and hosted an exhibit which traveled to several states. The Trust has at times, included barns in its annual listing of the most endangered places. Several state barn organizations now offer their own competitive programs to celebrate, appreciate, educate, and encourage sensible barn preservation.

In January 2013, the Smithsonian Institution, the world's largest museum and research complex, based in Washington, DC, launched a project to gather and exhibit materials documenting American farm and ranch history. Offered in partnership with the American Farm Bureau Federation, a nationwide organization of people working in agriculture, the exhibit—American Enterprise—is divided into four periods. It begins in the 1770s with the start of a market economy, captures the move from a rural society to a more urbanized one, examines a consumer-driven workplace, and is capped by globalization. People across the nation are contributing photographs, stories, and items illustrative of this extraordinary history for which the traditional barn plays an unquestionable role.

It will not be possible to save every barn but if people exercise good judgment by doing everything in their power to take good care of and make good use of a barn they have, find a new home for a barn they cannot keep, document barns when possible, or become an advocate for a barn in danger, the extraordinary structure that best symbolizes the heart not just of America's farms and ranches but America's spirit and resilience will live on.

The frame of this nineteenth-century barn has been dismantled, repaired, and raised again at Tillers International, a sustainable farming community in Scotts, Michigan, to enjoy another hundred years of life.

A barn owner stands in the center bay of a traditional English barn being dismantled for relocation.

PLACES TO VISIT

This list includes only a few of the many fascinating barn-related sites across the United States. Many more can be found by searching online (see www.nps.gov for many in national parks), reading the books cited in Further Reading, contacting the National Barn Alliance and state barn groups, and exploring America's back roads. Check for seasonal hours and special events before visiting.

ALASKA
Breeden Barn, Museum of Alaska Transportation and History, Wasilla
Stand inside the Breeden Barn (shown on pages 20 and 37), be amazed at its craftsmanship, and learn how it was given new life.

ARIZONA
OK Corral Stables, Tombstone
Experience "Wild wild west" history and click your heels at the Apache Spirit Ranch barn dance.

CALIFORNIA
Benicia Arsenal

Barns used to house livestock and store hay in Alabama. Note the rooflines.

First used as a military reserve, the 1855 barns stabled the only military "Camel Corps." Today they are part of a fascinating museum.

Point Reyes National Seashore
Nearly 300 structures including barns, lighthouses, and more represent the maritime and ranching culture of the central California coast.

CONNECTICUT

Weir Farm National Historic Site, Branchville
Home to three generations of Weir family artists, this site features a home, studios, barns, gardens, and pond nestled in a landscape of American art.

DELAWARE

Blue Ball Barn, Wilmington
Built in 1914 by Alfred DuPont, this barn in Alapocas Run State Park enjoys multiple lives in its adaptive reuse, including a large display of folk art.

INDIANA

Amish Acres, Nappanee
Created from 80 acres of an Old Order Amish Farm. Here you can savor a threshers' dinner and enjoy its Round Barn Theatre.

IOWA

Henry Moore's Mini-Americana Barn Museum, South Amana and West Amana barns
Be captivated by a rural Iowa community in miniature, complete with various barns, all inside a heritage horse barn. Visit the Communal Agriculture Museum and travel West Amana to see working Amana Colony barns.

KANSAS

Fromme-Birney Hexadecagon Barn, Mullinville
This awe-inspiring sixteen-sided barn was built in 1912 and one of only a few of its kind open to the public.

Native Stone Scenic Byway
Marvelous limestone barns and fences dot a 48-mile scenic route.

Flint Hills National Scenic Byway
See many extraordinary barns and homes dating from the late nineteenth and early twentieth century. Group tours available.

KENTUCKY

South Union Shaker Village, Auburn
Tour the five restored buildings of a 500-acre farm preserving the Shaker way of life.

Kentucky Bourbon Trail
Visit seven historic distilleries (taste if you wish) while your eyes drink in Kentucky's scenic back roads and landmark barns.

MASSACHUSETTS
Shaker Village Round Barn, Pittsfield
The only truly round barn (three stories high) ever built by Shakers, it used to house fifty-two cows and remains part of a working farm.

MICHIGAN
Castle Farms, Charlevoix
Restored castle-like barns (shown on page 18) which once housed cattle for a business executive who lived in his own castle on the grounds, and are now a popular wedding venue.
Gilmore Auto Museum, Hickory Corners
A visit satisfies both the lover of antique and rare autos and rare barns as well, including the five-story Campania mint barn, saved from demolition and moved here.
Thumb Octagon Barn Agricultural Museum, Gagetown
Saved from demolition, this barn is a work of art and the site of many events throughout the year hosted by its nearly 800 "Friends." A must-see in Michigan.

NEBRASKA
Wessels Living History Farm, Lincoln
David Wessels was a visionary when he willed that land and money be set aside to create a living history farm. Learn about farming from the 1920s to today.

NEW HAMPSHIRE
Poore Family Farm, Stewartstown
Step back in time to witness the life of the Poore family from the 1830s to the 1980s. Enjoy historical demonstrations, concerts, and picnics.

"The Heart of Heatherbrook Farm" mural features at its center an image of the barn on which it is mounted near Marshall, Michigan.

A traditional Swedish barn in Michigan's Upper Peninsula.

NEW YORK

Cooperstown Farmers Museum

This memorable historic village is made up of painstakingly restored homes, businesses, and barns important to rural life in the late eighteenth and early nineteenth centuries.

MaBee Farm Historic Site, Rotterdam Junction

The Nilsen Barn relocated to this site is a magnificent example of a Dutch barn and is believed to have been built in the 1760s. The barn has unique features.

Old Stone Fort Museum, Schoharie

Two stately old barns are included on the grounds of this Revolutionary War battle site where New York's beautiful Schoharie Valley is celebrated.

NORTH CAROLINA

Mast Farm Inn, Valle Crucis

Nestled in beautiful countryside, Mast Farm invites visitors to let go of the fast pace of life. Those who love unusual barns will want to have a camera along.

Mountain Farm Museum and Minges Mill, Oconaluftee

Some eighty mountain structures have been gathered from the Great Smokey Mountains to form this heritage-rich site. Check www.nps.gov for details and road conditions.

NORTH DAKOTA

Bagg Bonanza Farm, Mooreton

Bonanza farming is a term not often seen in American historical accounts and rarer still is the restoration of an entire farm having twenty-one buildings.

OHIO
Malabar Farm, Lucas
Louis Bromfield was a Pulitzer Prize-winning author and agricultural innovator. His beloved farm with its much-studied Sweitzer bank barn and carefully preserved home delights, informs, and provokes thought about history, architecture, and determination.

PENNSYLVANIA
Gettysburg National Memorial Park
Historic Brandywine Battlefield, Chadds Ford
Barns that survived the Civil War are part of the soul-touching legacy of this dark time in the country's history of the 1860s.

SOUTH DAKOTA
Little Village Farm Museum, Dell Rapids
Features eight restored buildings including five different types of barns each with period materials from 1860 to 1940.

TENNESSEE
National Parks
Visit the National Park Service website to learn about farmsteads and historic structures at Cades Cove, Cataloochee, the Museum of Appalachia, and the Roaring Fork Motor Nature Trail. Road conditions in the Great Smokey Mountains will be posted.

Cantilevered double-crib also known as an Appalachian overhung-loft barn in Tennessee.

UTAH
Historic Barns of Northern Utah
Contact the Bear River Heritage Area for a self-guided tour map and book.

VERMONT
Bread & Puppet Museum & Theatre, Glover
Be prepared for anything as you explore this old barn filled with creative, creepy characters.
Joslin Round Barn Farm, Waitsfield
Beautiful collection of well-loved farm buildings dating from 1860 to the 1930s, including a 1910 polygonal barn. The barn is home to the Green Mountain Cultural Center.
Morgan Horse Farm, University of Vermont, Middlebury
Home to more than sixty years of Morgan Horse history and an architecturally rare horse barn (show on page 18).
Shelburne Farms
National Historic Landmark. Stay onsite and be mesmerized by sustainable farming at its finest.
Shelburne Museum
Amazing round barn that displays firearms from the 1790s, unique fashions, circus memorabilia and much more, set on 45 acres with thirty-eight additional buildings to explore.

WASHINGTON
Sutton Barn, Eastern Washington University, Cheney
Began its life in 1884 for farming, became a classroom building in 1974 and now houses campus safety.
Hans Berthusen Barn, Lynden
Recently restored and open to the public, this 1887 barn has a rich history.

WISCONSIN
Chase Stone Barn, Chase
One of the last standing fieldstone barns and likely the biggest, its "Friends" have carried out a massive restoration project to make it an agricultural museum in its own park (shown on page 59).

WYOMING
Mormon Row Barns, Jackson Hole
Six heritage farmsteads in the Grand Teton National Park create a stunning photo opportunity. Late summer and early fall are peak times to visit.
Marysville Pony Express Barn
This unique stone barn was leased to the Pony Express in 1860 as one of the "home stations" between St. Joseph, Missouri and Sacramento, California. It is now a museum.

GLOSSARY

Adobe	Clay mixed with straw and sun-dried to form a brick.
Auger	Tool for piercing and boring.
Barn curtains	Composite fabric used to protect animals or crops from weather.
Bay	Section of barn between major framing units of posts and beams (bents).
Bent	Vertical posts joined with horizontal and braced members. A series of bents forms a frame.
Brace	Diagonal mortised timber at right angles to post and beam for strength.
Cantilevered or **forebay**	The second floor projects beyond the ground floor. Of Swiss and German origin.
Chinking	Material used to fill space.
Crib barn	Ventilated storage enclosure usually for corn or grain.
Gambrel roof	Roof with a double slope, the lower steeper than the upper.
Gin pole	Anchored vertical pole fixed with block and tackle to assist with barn raising.
Girt	Major horizontal structural component between posts.
Gothic/rainbow roof	An architectural design from medieval Europe revived in America between 1830 and 1890.
H-bent	The distinctive center aisle framing in a three-aisle Dutch barn in which the ends of the horizontal beam protrude through the vertical posts.
Hay carrier	First patented in 1867, these devices (there were more than 8,000 designs) traveled on a wood or metal rail mounted to the barn ridge and moved slings, forks, or tongs holding hay across the barn for storage.
Hay hood	A peak extending from a barn's gable end usually sheltering the hay carrier.
Haymow	Area of barn where hay is stored.
Hex signs	Colorful geometric patterns of German origin.
Hoop house	A tube-like shelter consisting of plastic or fabric over a bowed metal frame.

King post	A vertical support rising from a horizontal beam to the apex of the roof.
Laminated dimensional lumber	Layered wood of predetermined, precut size.
Log barns	Structures built from the entire trunks or sections of trees and notched to fit together.
Mortise and tenon	Wood joinery in which a slot is cut (mortise) in one piece to receive a projected member (tenon) of another and then held together with a peg.
Notch	A v-shaped cut that receives a matching cut for a secure fit.
Peg	Carved wooden device. Secures mortise and tenon joinery, also called a treenail.
Pentice	Shallow, sloping roof attached to an outer wall below the eaves, also called a pent roof.
Pike pole	A sapling with a spike in one end to jab into the frame as a bent is being raised to an upright position.
Plate	Horizontal timber connecting the tops of outside posts in bents.
Pole buildings	Dimensional lumber framing covered with sheet metal, quick to erect.
Purlin	Horizontal timber parallel to the rafter plate and ridge for stability and support.
Queen posts	A pair of vertical posts placed symmetrically on a tie beam, rising to the principal rafters.
Rafters	Light, dimensional timber to which roofing materials are attached.
Shawver truss	A type of barn frame construction designed by John Shawver, which allows for greater spans and uses less lumber.
Shingles	Small sections of slate, wood, or a composite used to cover a roof.
Siding	Outer wall covering.
Sill or **sill plate**	Long horizontal timbers laid on the foundation to bear the floor joists and support the posts and studs of the frame.
Silo	A vertical cylindrical structure of wood stave, stone, block, tile or metal for the storage of animal fodder.
Stick and daub	A type of material used to fill spaces between studs. May be saplings or sticks (wattle)

	or horsehair (daub). Also known as wattle and daub.
Story pole	A long section of wood on which important measurements are marked.
Stovewood/ cordwood	Lengths of cedar (usually 16 inch) laid in a limestone mortar to serve as the foundation and sometimes entire walls of a structure.
Swing beam	A beam large enough to span the width of a barn without interior support posts. So named because a team of horses could then "swing" or be turned inside the barn.
Timber frame/ post and beam	The supportive skeleton of a structure built with solid timber using mortise, tenon and pegged construction rather than dimensional lumber.
Transverse crib barn	A gable entrance barn with two rows of animal stalls on either side of a central aisle with the haymow or hayloft over the stalls.

FURTHER READING

Bernhardt, Marcia and Harold. *Barns, Farms and Yarns.* Iron County Museum, Caspian, Michigan, 1999.

Brown, David G. *The American Farm: A Vanishing Way of Life.* Key Porter Books, Toronto, Ontario, 1998.

Crittendon, Bob. *Barn in the U.S.A.* Fulcrum Publishing, Golden Colorado, 2006.

Davis, Jerry R. *Barns from the Land of Enchantment.* Artemesia Publishing, Tijeras, New Mexico, 2012.

Endersby, Greenwood, and Larkin. *Barn. The Art of a Working Building.* Houghton Mifflin Company, New York, New York, 1992.

Endersby, Greenwood, and Larkin. *Barn Preservation & Adaptation. The Evolution of a Vernacular Icon.* Universe Publishing, New York, New York, 2003.

Frydenlund, Bob and Kathy. *How to Build & Love Your Own Round Barn.* Dry Creek Press, New Richmond, Wisconsin, 2000.

Frydenlund, Bob and Kathy. *The Original Round Barn Building Plan Book.* Dry Creek Press, New Richmond, Wisconsin, 2003.

Gray, Pamela Whitney. *Americanization of the Family Barn.* Gray's Venture, Mount Vernon, Ohio, 2009.

Hoogterp, Edward. *Working Assets for Sustainable Farms*. National Trust for Historic Preservation, 2007.

Hubka, Thomas C. *Big House, Little House, Back House, Barn. The Connected Farm Buildings of New England*. University Press of New England, 2004.

Hunter, Rebecca L. *Mail-Order Homes, Sears Homes and Other Kit Houses*. Shire Publications, Oxford, 2012.

Leffingwell, Randy. *Barns*. MBI Publishing Company. St. Paul, Minnesota, 2001.

Leffingwell, Randy. *The American Barn*. Motorbooks International, St. Paul, Minnesota, 2003.

Metro Books. *Barns*. Michael Friedman Publishing Group, Inc., New York, New York, 2001.

Noble, Allen G. and Cleek, Richard K. *The Old Barn Book. A Field Guide to North American Barns & Other Farm Structures*. Rutgers University Press, New Brunswick, New Jersey, sixth printing, 2007.

Osterud, Grey. *Putting the Barn Before the House: Women and Family Farming in Early Twentieth-Century New York*. Cornell University Press, Ithaca and London, 2012.

Peters, J. E. C. *Discovering Traditional Farm Buildings*. Shire Publications, Oxford, 1981.

Radojkovic, Jon. *Barn Building The Golden Age of Barn Construction*. Boston Mills Press, Erin, Ontario, 2007.

Reiman, Roy J. *This Old Barn*. Reiman Publications, Greendale, Wisconsin, 1996.

Sayward, Elliot, Feriola, James, and Johnson, Leonard G. *Of Plates and Purlins, Grandpa builds a barn*. The Early Trades and Crafts Society and the Friends of the Nassau County Museum, Long Island, New York, 1971.

Sears, Roebuck and Co., Chicago. *The Book of Barns*. A reprint of the 1919 catalog, 2005.

Sloane, Eric. *An Age of Barns*. Voyageur Press, 2001.

The Mount Vernon Ladies' Association. *George Washington: Pioneer Farmer*. A dedication booklet, 1996.

Viola, Herman. *After Columbus. The Smithsonian Chronicle of the North American Indians*. The Smithsonian Institution, 1990.

Visser, Thomas Durant. *Field Guide to New England Barns and Farm Buildings*. University Press of New England, 1997.

Vlach, John Michael. *Barns*. Norton/Library of Congress Visual Sourcebooks in Architecture, Design, and Engineering. W. W. Norton & Company, New York and London; Library of Congress, Washington DC, 2003.

Wilkinson, Christina. *Bicentennial Barns*. Rosewood Press, Ohio, 2003.

Witzel, Michael Karl. *Barns: Styles & Structures*. Motorbooks International, St. Paul, Minnesota, 2003.

INDEX

Page numbers in italics refer to
illustrations

Advertising on barns
3, 20
Alabama 62
Alaska 20, 37
Algonquin Indian 5
American pioneer 10
Amish 20, 26, 34
Appalachian Meadow
barn 21
Appalachian overhung
loft barn 11, 66
Arkansas 12
Balloon-frame 21, 27
Bank barn 10
Barn preservation
campaigns/
organisations 11,
16, 17, 41, 56,
57, 58, 59, 60
Bauernhaus 23, 56
Books 13, 15, 17, 20,
23, 26, 39, 58, 60
Cantilevered double-
crib barn 66
Cantilevered forebay
barn 10, 13, 20
Colorado 27
Connected barns 13,
13, 23, 24
Connecticut 30
Cordwood barns 11, 11
Crib barn 30
Crib-log barns 17
Dairy barns 4, 29
Dakota Territory 27
Decahexagonal barns 15
Deere, John 42
Depression barns 11
Double-crib barn 11
Dust Bowl 43
Dutch barn 6, 7, 8, 23
Dutch-American 13

English barn 7, 17,
56, 61
Europe 5, 6, 26, 57
Franklin, Benjamin
26, 47
Gambrel-roofed barn
4, 9, 27, 29, 53
Georgia barn 11
German barn 7, 10,
23, 56
Gothic-roofed 28, 29
Great Depression
11, 43
Great Plains 43
Hawaiian islands 44
Hexagonal barns 15
Hispanic influence 13
Homestead Act 26
Housebarns 23
Illinois 8, 11, 29, 39
Indiana 14
Intermountain barns 12
Immigrants/settlers:
Dutch 6; English 6;
Finnish 11, 25;
French 17; German
25, 57, 59; Irish 17;
Italians 17; Scottish
17; Spanish 25;
Swedish 11, 25; Swiss
25; Ukranian 23
Iowa 14, 56
Jefferson, Thomas
26, 27
Kansas, 26, 27
Kentucky 16, 17
Kit barns 38, 39,
39, 56
Log barn 10, 11, 22–3,
24, 33, 35, 36
Long Island 30
Louisiana 49
Maine 23, 35
McCormick, Cyrus 42
Mennonite 20

Michigan 6, 9, 11, 11,
12, 18, 22–3, 25, 29,
31, 38, 40, 48, 52,
54, 55, 60, 61, 64, 65
Milk houses 29
Minnesota 11, 25, 50
Missouri 41
Montana 17
Mormons 7
Morrill Act 29, 49
Mount Vernon 14, 15
Native Americans 5, 6,
13, 41
Nebraska 27, 37
New England 13, 23
New Hampshire 13
New Jersey 7
New Mexico 24
New World Dutch
barns 7
New York 7, 8, 56, 58
North Carolina 5, 16,
17, 54
North Dakota 25, 48
Oahu 44
Octagonal barn 14, 15
Ohio 15, 17, 19, 20,
21, 26, 28, 47, 53
Oregon 27
Oval barns 15
Pennsylvania 3, 10, 13,
18, 21, 25, 41:
forebay barns 17;
German barn 10;
Standard 10
Pentagonal barns 15
Plantation barns 13
Potato barn 30
Prairie barn 27
Rack-sided livestock
barn 15
Round barns 15
Rural Electrification
Act 30
Sears, Roebuck and
Company 39

Shawver truss 20, 21
Slice hip-roof barn 16
South America 5, 26
Stovewood barns 11
Successful Farming 60
Swedish barn 21
Sweitzer/Swisser 10
Swing-beam barns
13, 17
Tennessee 20, 46, 66
Texas 27, 41, 56
Timber-frame barn
5, 7, 33, 41, 51,
57, 59
Tithe barns 6, 7
Tobacco barns 16, 21
Transverse crib barn 11
United States
Department of
Agriculture 41, 54
Utah 7, 12
Vermont 18, 56
Virginia 10, 16, 17
Washington, George
14, 15, 17
Wisconsin 11, 18, 28,
41, 58, 59, 60
Wars 5, 26, 41, 43
Wyoming 27